The
Great Picture Hunt

The art and ethics of feature picture hunting

By Dave LaBelle
Western Kentucky University

Foreword by Larry Nighswander

To Chuck:
Thank you for the opportunity
to meet you. I wish you
the best with your photography
and your life. Shoot from the heart!
Dave LaBelle

The Great Picture Hunt

The art and ethics of feature photography

Library of Congress Catalog Number: 89-092287

ISBN   0-9630770-8-2

First edition, second printing 1991
Printed in the United States of America

All Photographs © by Dave LaBelle.
Edited by Rex Perry

For information write:
Dave LaBelle
Garrett Conference Center Room 220
Western Kentucky University
Bowling Green, Kentucky   42101

Dave LaBelle
493 Peachtree Lane
Bowling Green, Kentucky 42103
(502) 782-3619

Cover Photo: Proud parents and grandparents exhibit their babies before a panel of judges while standing in the hot sun July the fourth in Altoona, Kan.

Acknowledgements

Layout: Rex Perry and Dave LaBelle

Copy editors:
Bob Adams
Jo-Ann Albers
James Ausenbaugh
Betty Jarboe Powell
Lisa Jessie

A special thanks to Betty Powell for her encouragement, coaching and the numerous hours she spent editing and typing, and to Rex Perry for his unselfish contribution of time and energy. Thanks go to George Wedding for dropping everything during a busy schedule to write the foreword for the first printing. Without your help this book would never have happened.

Artwork for making a tree is by Lisa Mauer.
Back cover photograph by Elane Cash
Author photograph on page 92 by Larry Powell

Table of contents

Foreword

Webster's New Collegiate Dictionary describes photography as the art or process of producing images on a sensitized surface. Unfortunately, Webster's dictionary lacked the space to differentiate between the art and process in its application to photography.

Too frequently photographers exhibit the process and not the art in their photographic vision. Dave LaBelle is an advocate for the use of the brain, the heart and the eyes in photography. This is evidenced in the photographs he has taken during his extensive career as a photojournalist.

The fact that he has chosen to share his experience and his mindset with all of us is further evidence of the altruistic passion that he has for photography and life.

Reading The Great Picture Hunt will open many eyes. It will remind you of the joys and sorrows, the laughs and tears and the broad range of emotions we all feel as we experience life. The skills and thought processes it takes to visually capture those moments are logically presented on the pages of this book.

Besides the information needed to fine tune your sense of photographic timing, you get the added bonus of seeing the wonderful moments LaBelle has captured with his camera.

A camera is a powerful tool. Coupled with an attentive mind, photography becomes a powerful medium.

I hope you find great joy in "hunting" for those pictures that make our world the special place in which we live.

Larry Nighswander
National Geographic magazine

To my family, Joyce, Charbonee and Bergen
for their sacrifices and support.

Introduction

As a photojournalist, I have weaknesses. I am an average sports shooter, a decent breaking-news photographer and weak studio photographer. But I am not without some ability. I am an idea person, with more picture ideas to shoot than time to shoot them. I love shooting picture stories. But of my talents, perhaps finding and shooting features is what I do best. I am a feature photographer at heart.

Since taking a leave of absence from shooting full time to join the faculty at Western Kentucky University, I have found that even though enterprising is an integral part of the job for most photojournalists, it is something most students are not taught much about. Furthermore, it is a responsibility that most actually hate. Give a student an assignment – an idea with a location – and the majority will return with decent pictures. Send them out to enterprise and they seem lost and unsure where to begin. It was this discovery that motivated me to assemble this book.

Growing up I spent countless hours hunting the hills and creeks. What to hunt never seem to matter much. It was the thrill of just being out with nature and trying to outwit whatever it was I was chasing that mattered. Although I seldom hunt anymore because I hate to kill anything, I learned many lessons from those years in the woods that taught me to be a better hunter with a camera.

The publishing world today has an enormous appetite for high-quality feature photographs. Newspapers, newsletters, magazines and advertising agencies are all hungry for and depend greatly on feature photography. But what do you look for in a feature picture? What are its qualities? And how do you find them once you know what you are looking for? The answers are not as simple as they may seem.

Like stalking wild game or unearthing hidden treasure, shooting good feature pictures is a form of hunting that requires instinct and skill.

Occasionally pictures will just happen, and bagging the quarry is not difficult. But more often than not, finding those elusive feature pictures is like trying to pick a pair of brown socks in the dark – not an easy task.

Enterprising usually means finding something interesting, well-composed, timely and maybe even meaningful – on deadline. The hunt can be a refreshing escape from a hectic newsroom, or it can be a gut-wrenching, pressure-packed search that leaves you frustrated, angry and emotionally drained.

When you are successful in finding something even remotely worthy of publication, you are somewhat of a journalastic hero. But when you return to the office empty-handed past deadline, you are the goat – the field goal kicker who misses a chip shot and loses the game for the entire team.

Feature hunting is not easy. Like playing the piano or painting, it is an acquired skill, an art form that requires desire, study and never-ending practice.

Chapter 1

Hunter Qualities

What makes a good feature hunter?

Just as big game hunters consistently return from excursions with trophy animals, some photographers consistently return to the office with interesting feature pictures. Some photojournalists are better enter- prisers (feature photo hunters) while others are better in the studio. But why is it so, particularly when the desires to be a good enterpriser and have technical ability are often similar? Is it just luck that seems to always lead one photographer to be in the right place at the right time? Of course not.

There are, in fact, clear reasons why some photographers are better feature hunters than others. In this chapter, I have marked five distinct qualities I believe separate the average feature hunters from the great ones. Some of those qualities are learned, and some are natural.

Curious

Natural feature hunters are inherently curious. They are the type of people who as children tore apart old television sets to find out where the pictures came from.

Curiosity: It is a photographer's best friend and greatest asset. You can teach many things, but you cannot teach curiosity. It is something you are born with. It is the very soul of a good enterprising journalist.

Curiosity is the passion that drives photographers to search beneath the skin of life to discover more than just what something looks like, but also what it smells like, tastes like, sounds like, acts like, feels like and, most importantly, what it means.

Good photojournalists are not in love with photography, they are in love with people and with life. For them photography is a tool, a vehicle for communication to open doors to the world and then carry back their discoveries.

Blending

Skilled hunters don't crash through the woods with guns blazing or overload themselves with unnecessary gear. On the contrary, they move quietly and carefully so as not to attract attention or frighten off game. They **blend** with the environment.

Seasoned feature hunters are no different. Their goal is not to disrupt society or impress others with their flashy dress, fancy cars or expensive camera equipment, but to capture the prey – those candid moments in life. They do this with a minimum of interruption, usually by blending in with the environment.

Like black panthers in the dark, truly good feature photographers silently stalk their prey.

Prepared

As the adage goes, "Even a blind hog finds an ear of corn now and then." An unprepared novice hunter can stumble upon game occasionally, but the veteran hunter, the one who consistently comes home with his bag limits, does so because he is **prepared**. He knows his quarry – where it lives, where it eats and when it sleeps. Furthermore, he can tell you where it is likely to be and what it does at any given time of the day.

A good feature hunter consistently produces interesting pictures because he works at it and is prepared. As some have said, "Luck is nothing more than preparation meeting opportunity."

Just as the seasoned hunter prepares for the unexpected by packing maps, matches, extra fuel or cartridges, good photojournalists also should prepare by carrying certain items to increase their odds for a successful and safe hunt. Suggestions for better preparation include:

• **Always keep film in your cameras**. This is a must. Too many great pictures have been shot on invisible film. The best policy is to load your cameras as soon as you unload them.

• **Keep an emergency roll of film**. Inevitably something great will happen, maybe even the most story-telling picture, after you have fired your last frame on your last roll. If you have to, hide a roll somewhere in your car, as you might a $20 bill. Thirty-six frames of Tri-X tucked away might win you that Pulitzer Prize.

• **Save a few frames at the end of each roll**. Even if you think you have go what you need from a shoot, keep an emergency few frames at the end of your last roll for grab shots.

• **Keep a pen/pencil and a note pad**. Many good ideas are lost because they are forgotten. A note pad should be in your bag, car and at work.

• **Keep your cameras set**. Many times there isn't even a second to change lenses or adjust exposures before the moment vanishes By remembering to pre-set your cameras on automatic or at a reasonable outdoor setting, you will be prepared for those unexpected pictures.

It is also a good practice to keep your cameras equipped with two contrasting focal lengths. I like to keep a 24mm and a 300mm handy, but a wide-angle to medium focal-length zoom lens also would do the trick. It wouldn't hurt if one of the cameras were an autofocus, either.

• **Keep a tripod**. A tripod is an essential tool for any photographer, particularly when shooting color.

• **Keep gas in your car**. Keep enough fuel in your car at all times to get you at least 50 miles and back. It never fails that when you need to get

somewhere in a hurry, your gauge is on empty. Sometimes there isn't time to stop for gas or there are no stations around. Obviously this is a greater problem in Kansas or North Dakota than in California.

• **Keep extra cash**. There are times when credit cards are not practical. By stashing a little money in your camera bag or automobile glove box you will be prepared for emergencies like coffee, phones, tips or bribes.

• **Keep a map**. Maps are essential things to have. It is easy to wander and get lost when you're feature hunting in new territory.

• **Camera bag goodies**. A spare set of car keys, extra batteries, earplugs, a plastic bag (to keep film and camera dry), credit cards, tape, synch cords, a knife, a small screwdriver kit, pliers and a multi-purpose pocketknife that has a screwdriver and scissors are nearly standard requirements for the prepared photographer.

• **Emergency aids**. A blanket, rope, bandages, chain, jumper cables, flares, spare tire and jack can be stowed away for an emergency.

• **Other items to keep in your car**. A raincoat, a working flashlight, toilet paper, a toothbrush, a change of clothes and maybe some canned food. You never know where your cameras will take you.

Needing to share

The best feature photographers are story tellers. They have a burning **need to share** what they see and discover in life to feel fulfilled. For them feature hunting isn't a dreaded chore, it's an opportunity to examine life and visually shout out what they find interesting or important.

Within me there is such a need. It is an abiding call that I seem unwilling or unable to ignore. The poignant life experiences I live and observe seem so empty and incomplete if I am unable to share them.

Perhaps it is this need that really separates the photographers from the photojournalists, or the artist from the technician. Call it ambition, ego or simply the need, it is a real and powerful force that drives many photojournalists.

Patient

Truly great feature hunters are, above all, **patient**. The photographer who thinks he can pop in and out of picture situations and shoot great moments is mistaken. Good photographs are seldom hanging around to be plucked like apples on a tree. Most often, the compelling images – the meaningful moments – are the result of a considerable time investment and tremendous patience.

Like a cat poised motionless over a gopher hole, you might have to sit or stand for long periods of time – maybe even hours – until the picture happens. This requires great concentration and more mental and physical energy than you might imagine. Sometimes, despite your preparation and patience, the picture never quite seems to materialize, and you go home empty-handed and worn out.

Of all the feature photographer's enemies, time is the greatest adversary. With it, you can wait for the moment to happen. Without it, you are like an investor forced to cash a bond before maturity.

Photographing real, candid moments isn't easy. If it were, anybody could do it. To be a good feature hunter you need time and patience, and there just is no substitute for either.

Chapter 2

Learning To Hunt

What makes a good feature photograph?

Before hunters of any game can hope to capture a trophy animal, they must know what that animal looks like. What qualities distinguish it as a trophy?

Good feature hunters should be no different. They should know what makes a good feature picture and what one looks like before setting out to capture it. Nothing is more important in a feature picture than for it to be visually interesting.

Interest, like being good, is a subjective term depending greatly upon the eyes and interest of the viewer. But there are tangible qualities or common characteristics that most interesting photographs share.

Key virtues most good feature photographs have are **emotion**, **moments**, **simplicity**, **composition,** unusual **angles**, captivating **subject matter**, **humor**, arousing **technique** and **originality**. Look for these qualities in a picture when you go hunting and you will be more successful.

Emotion

It has been proven over and over again that people like to see others working, playing, winning and losing. Pictures that show people, or the "human condition," are pictures that usually show **emotion**.

In journalism, pictures lacking emotion usually are lifeless, even boring. As a reader you see them and say, "So what? Why did they publish that picture?" But when we see human emotion played out in pictures, we identify with the subjects of those pictures.

Images that are alive with emotion talk to readers. They say something. They move us with humor or empathy, and cause us as readers to react and become involved. When this happens there is communication, that rare and wonderful happening that every journalist aims for.

See how many emotions you can visualize: fear, love, hate, joy, depression, empathy, despair, sympathy, pride, embarassment, boredom. Just making a mental list of some common emotions should start your creative wheels turning.

Study your favorite pictures and you will find they are filled with emotion.

Top: Seven-year-old Cathy Whitworth's face is filled with emotion as she encourages her lamb to pay attention while livestock judges aren't looking. Left: Big faces are important to show emotion. Some publications insist that there be a big face in every issue of their publication.

Moments

Moments. They are the very heart and soul of documentary photojournalism. Some are national or international happenings seen and heard across the world, but most are not. Most are small, quiet local events in everyday life that get little attention.

For me, nothing is more interesting or compelling in a photograph than a real moment – that magic time when all of the elements, like bars on a slot machine, come together to pay pictorial dividends.

But what is a moment? It is a fragment of life that speaks of a person's or animal's character. Unlike a portrait, which is a controlled likeness of the person's outer being, a moment captures more of a person's inner likeness.

Moments make statements – they say something about the human condition. They don't require poetic words to describe to the reader what is happening, only identification of the subject and the circumstances.

A moment can be a look, a touch, a gesture or a

A moment is that magic time when all the elements, like bars on a slot machine, come together to pay pictorial dividends. It is a storytelling slice of life, like this photograph of children eagerly awaiting the start of a pie-eating contest.

combination of all. They are fleeting capsules of life, usually found at the crest of an emotional wave. As photojournalists, we use these fragments of a greater whole to tell the story of an event, or at least to represent what we feel about it.

Life is a collection of millions of moments happening constantly. Deciding what moment best embodies the pulse or essence of a story is a personal matter. What moments we choose to shoot and share speak of our individuality, as photojournalists and as human beings.

Norman Rockwell didn't paint pictures; he painted moments. I don't want to shoot pictures that just record life or document history. I try to dig deeper to show readers more than what a person or a thing looks like. I try to show them what it acts like, feels like and what it means. There is a difference.

Shooting moments also requires having a point of view. Henri Cartier-Bresson said it well. "Facts are not interesting. It is the point of view on facts that is interesting."

This picture of 6-year-old Nicole Haley competing in a 25-yard breast stroke race is uncluttered and easy to read. You don't have to hunt for the message; communication is immediate.

Simplicity

Sometimes a picture has good subject matter and a moment is taking place, but the moment is lost because the photograph is too cluttered or busy. Unnecessary background or foreground detail makes looking for the subject like trying to find a canary in a banana tree.

When you consider that readers are bombarded daily with hundreds, maybe thousands, of visual opportunities, the value of pictures that tell stories quickly is clear. If we are going to compete with television with our one-dimensional, still photographs, we need to keep our images clean and our message **simple**. One of my mentors, Robert E. Clark, said it best. "We need to respect the readers' time."

Simple, uncluttered images, on the other hand, are easy to read because the reader doesn't have to hunt for the message. These pictures are called "quick reads," and they are almost a must in photo competitions.

Though really a guideline of composition, sim-

plicity in feature photographs is such a neglected tool to attract reader attention that I felt it deserved special mention here.

Easy-to-read pictures can be achieved in many ways. Sometimes all it takes to clean up those backgrounds is to bend your knees or change angles. Try using longer lenses with wider apertures to eliminate unwanted background detail, or get closer to your subjects with shorter focal lengths. Avoid backgrounds that are the same shape, tone or color as your subjects, particularly with black-and-white film. Look for contrasts that will help the reader see quicker, like dark subjects against light backgrounds or vice versa.

Not all feature pictures can be simple and clean, nor should they be. Some pictures need backgrounds to tell the story, but many times feature pictures happen so quickly there is no time to clean them up without losing the moment. Those times are the exceptions, not the rule. Remember, simple is best.

Composition

Many pictures are interesting solely because of their compelling patterns, poetic lines or enchanting shapes and tones – in short, their **composition**.

In feature photography, composition (how the elements of a picture are arranged) is critical to attracting readers. With the exceptions of moments and subject matter, no aspect of feature photography is more important to making pictures interesting.

The homes we live in, the highways we drive on, the clothes we wear are all designed with composition in mind. Feature pictures should be no different.

As a feature photographer, you are the artist, the director, the composer. You decide what and where subjects and elements will be arranged in your photographs.

I heard a preacher once say that character is the sum total of the decisions we make in our lives. Your individuality as a photographer is expressed by the decisions you make about the arrangement in the viewfinder.

To learn more about composition, pick up a good book on the subject. Nearly every thorough basic photography book gives extensive space to the study of composition. Better yet, spend some time walking downtown or in the forest and study the arrangement of the world around you. There are design and composition everywhere.

Lines, shapes, tones and scale work together to attract reader interest and create mood in this image of a man leaving a Utah hospital late in the evening.

There is little doubt that this photograph of a salmon jumping nose–first into a cement fish ladder in Anchorage, Alaska won first place for feature picture in the 1977 Pictures of the Year contest because it was different.

Originality

Difference goes a long way toward being interesting. Most of us get bored, and when something unusual or different comes along, even something weird or off the wall, our curiosity is stirred and we become interested. It is that way in life, and it is that way in photography. Although going against the norm is risky, doing so is usually noticed. Difference, good or bad, attracts attention.

I have judged many photo competitions, some with thousands of prints, and after just a few hours of scrutinizing, pictures begin to look alike. You get mesmerized by the quantity and repetition. Often before judging is over, you find yourself punch drunk and maybe even a little weird or cynical. You ache for something new, fresh, unusual – **origina**l.

When a picture cries out and says, "Look at me. I'm different," you nearly fall over yourself, sometimes to the point of overreacting.

To grab my attention: Stop me, excite me and surprise me. Tickle my curiosity and whet my visual appetite with something different.

There may not be any new ideas under the sun, but there certainly are many new ways to look at them.

Humor

What would life be without **humor**? It is a special gift to carry us through some of life's most difficult times. As evidenced by the great success of the "Candid Camera" television show, we enjoy seeing ourselves and others in amusing predicaments.

For me, humor is at the core of feature photography. Though often accused of having a weird sense of humor, I am always on the lookout for pictures that will make people laugh. Feature photographs portraying humor break up the unpleasant or painful news, offering readers a momentary escape.

But a word of caution about feature photos with a humorous twist: Be careful not to unduly embarrass or poke fun at subjects. It is easy to be insensitive in this area and have a public laugh at the expense of a private individual.

Keep a sense of humor, but be very cautious. What is funny to one person may not be funny to the next.

This picture of 3-year-old Glen Wilson temporarily trapped in a telephone booth. It has won widespread publication because it is rich with emotion and humor.

Olivia Newton John is vivacious on stage, but showing up several hours before her concert gave readers a quieter look at the famous singer who was fighting a cold.

Angle

Who can forget those first pictures of the earthrise shot by Apollo 8 astronaut William Anders while circling the moon in 1969?

When I first saw them I was overwhelmed. It gave me an eerie, uncomfortable feeling. Why? Like others, I had never seen the earth – my home – from that perspective before, and it felt funny.

In the same way, pictures from everyday places and events, when presented from a fresh vantage point, will grab attention and stir curiosity. Beyond changing camera angle, from low to high or back to front, consider changing the environment in which your pictures are shot. Take the reader off the field, and into the locker room.

Take a chance. Show readers something they can't see from their seats. Don't show them the same boring mug shots they see on television. A talking head on television is a dead head in a print publication.

Delight me. Excite me with revealing candid moments of people when they are off-camera and unaware of your presence. Show me a fresh **angle** of something old and I will look.

By taking readers to a vantage point they don't normally get to see, you can make a good picture situation even better as with the photograph of a child trying to reach a five dollar bill on a greased pole.

Subject Matter

There is a saying in the newspaper business that you can't make chicken salad out of chicken droppings. There is another camp of thought that says that good photographers, those with imagination, can make even the dullest assignment interesting. Though there is truth to both positions, there simply is no substitute for good **subject matter**.

With good subject matter (interesting faces, lively happenings or poignant moments), a monkey with an Instamatic can take an interesting picture. Beginning shooters, novices who hardly knew which end of the camera to point, have taken great, prize-winning photographs because great, visually interesting events were happening in front of them.

So it goes. What you shoot often is far more important than how you shoot it. Good photojournalists consider good subject matter a gift, then proceed to work it with their photographic and journalistic skills.

It wasn't diificult to shoot good pictures of Glen Mitchell trying to survive near a California creekbed. His face, clothing and environment alone make him visually interesting.

Let's face it, some people and events are more visually exciting than others. A 90-year-old woman who lives alone in the mountains raising goats usually will yield more interesting pictures than a man who operates a computer in an office.

Look at the daytime talk shows. Why are they so popular? Certainly much of their success is due to the subject matter they discuss. They exist on a foundation of abnormality: near-death experiences, serial kill-ers, sex changes and movie stars. With subject matter like that, who wouldn't be curious?

Much of my succcess as a feature photographer has resulted more from the unusual and interesting subjects I chose to photograph and my ability to gain access into their lives, than from any photographic skills I might possess. After all, the subject matter you choose often speaks loudly of your personality and style.

Top: Using a mirror to reflect a subject's image often is employed to create interest in a photograph as with this image of a paralyzed man who still enjoys riding his motorcycle. Bottom: Vignetting emphasizes the deep facial lines of the subject..

Technique

Sometimes technique attracts attention and renders a picture interesting: the use of a filter, the slowing of a shutter, how a picture is printed, the use of creative lighting, the incorporation of a specialty lens such as a fish eye or soft focus.

As Gary Chapman of The Courier-Journal in Louisville puts it, "Every picture has a star, and sometimes that star is the **technique**."

In documentary photography, it is important that the technique doesn't overshadow, change the picture's message or steal the star status from the content. Shooting or printing techniques should quietly lend support to the photographer's message.

Left: St. Paul, Kan., basketball player, Keith Van Leeuwen leaps off the bench as a teammate sinks a winning freethrow with no time left on the clock. Below: Box Elder, Utah, wrestling coach, Lamoin Merkley, embraces one of his wrestlers after a state championship match.

Action and reaction

There are photographs that can reach right out from a newspaper box, grab readers' attention and stop them cold in their tracks. It has happened to me, not by some pretty, no-content, color picture or talking-head shot of a politician, but by raw action and reaction.

Expression, movement, consolation or confrontation in sports, news or feature pictures will turn a lot of heads. **Action and reaction** immediately involve and seduce a reader into wanting to know more. Think how many times have been doing

something and were frozen by the sight or sound of real action on television . Feature pictures that are alive with action and reaction speak loudly and arouse the eye. There is a visual excitement not found in the boring handshake or team pictures. There is a message being communicated, a feeling shared.

We are drawn to many pictures because of their colors, tones, arrangement. But in photojournalism, images with life and action usually get the most attention.

Finding people caring and sharing, such as this exchange between a swimming instructor and her handicapped student, will involve readers emotionally.

Interaction

Most of us look at pictures, be it paintings or photographs, without really giving much thought to why we are drawn to one image over another. Just liking a picture seems reason enough to look at it and enjoy it. But have you ever asked yourself what it is about a certain picture that makes it so compelling? I doubt many of us stop and really analyze why we are drawn to a particular photograph.

In studying some of my favorite pictures to determine what it was about them I found interest-ing, I have discovered that the pictures I enjoyed most were of people interacting – caring, sharing, helping or even fighting. And why not? Pictures that show people interacting with other people or with animals serve as mirrors to reflect and remind us of what we are as human beings. They show us what is good about ourselves, or what we would like to be, and what is lacking.

Images with strong subject interaction likely will interest most readers because they are about each of us and our relationship to each other.

Body language

A touch, the tilt of a head, the crossing of arms or even the posture one has while standing, can speak clearly about the way a person feels or sees himself. **Body language** is the act of non-verbally communication, and it is a quick and powerful, yet subtle, way of communicating.

Emotion usually is associated with facial expression, and we already have discussed the importance of big faces to capture reader interest, but there are instances when the back of a person can say as much as a face. Hands on hips, unabashed embraces, the crossing of one's legs – each stance says and means something to the reader when captured in pictures. Sometimes body language is quiet and hard to discern, while other body movements cry out with piercing declaration.

Body language can lend quiet support to facial expression, or it can speak its own message. Without ever seeing a face, a body can say hello or goodbye, leave me alone or I'd like to get to know you. Combine expressive faces with body language and the photograph becomes even more appealing because the message is unmistakably clear.

If you want your pictures to be more interesting, spend some time studying body language and what certain movements mean. Watch for that non-verbal language to help you communicate better through your feature photographs.

Some people show more visually interesting body language than others. Track starter, Harry Burchell and Mt. View Utah High School wrestling coach, Fred Rolland both show the distinct body language that makes photographs alive and interesting.

Chapter 3

Hunting Methods

How to find those elusive feature photographs.

Once a hunter has decided what game to pursue and what a trophy animal looks like, he will begin planning how to find his game.

Now that you know what to look for in good feature photo-graphs, your next step will be planning your strategy for finding them. To help you capture more of those elusive feature pictures, try these 12 time–tested methods that have worked for me.

1. Brainstorming

This photograph was published in the Muskogee (Okla.) Pheonix as part of a picture package on a family-owned sheep operation. The story idea resulted from a brainstorming session with lifestyle editor Susan Savage.

A method common to all aspects of journalism, photography not excluded, is **brainstorming**. It is the practice of getting together to share or generate story ideas with the belief that two heads are better than one.

Brainstorming can be part of a regular formal meeting, or it can be an informal gathering after hours. With brainstorming, the only bad ideas are the ones you keep to yourself.

Seek out reporters, editors, designers, ad salesmen, security guards or anyone willing to offer creative thinking. Ask reporters about stories they are working on and about story ideas they may be developing. Ask people outside the newsroom about issues that concern them or of interesting people they have met.

Talk with other photographers to learn about picture ideas they don't have time to work on but that need to be photographed. Build upon each other's ideas during brainstorming sessions. Word associations sometimes can help develop illustration ideas while brainstorming.

It is important that you make the first move to call these brainstorming sessions. Don't wait with your mouth open like a baby bird to be fed picture ideas. Take the initiative. Photographers are notorious for complaining about picture assignments or the lack of them, but only a few offer alternatives.

2. Cruising

The morning was typical. I had nothing in the way of art for that day's paper. I frantically canvassed town and country for pictures. I was **cruising**, searching for anything remotely resembling a feature photograph.

Already I had driven more than 70 miles in two hours and had nothing to show for it. The pressure to find something was building. My gas gauge was planted on empty, my stomach began to knot up and I grew more panicky by the minute. I was past deadline.

The pressure was incredible. Would this be the day, after two years of successfully "pulling a rabbit out of the hat," that I failed to return to the office with a publishable feature photo? The thought of failure made me sick. I kept looking. I had "buck fever." I was ready to shoot at anything: birds on a wire, dogs on a porch, anything.

Suddenly, almost magically, I caught a glimpse of something out of the ordinary. My heart pounded fast, like that of a baseball player struggling to keep a long hitting streak alive. I thumped the brake pedal hard and jerked the car into reverse all in one motion.

Was there really something to shoot or was I hallucinating?

Wait a minute! Yes, in a pile of trash the naked legs of a mannequin protruding from an old tractor tire. Bingo!

I breathed a thankful sigh of relief and quickly fired a few frames. It wasn't much, maybe even a little weird, but it was a picture.

When cruising for features, it is often the unusual that catches your eye, like a child rolling in an innertube in Chanute, Kan., or a goat appearing to read a sign in Layton, Utah.

At many newspapers, cruising often is the child of poor planning – a last-minute effort to find something for open pages. Without a doubt, cruising is the most common method used by photographers to produce feature photographs.

In Chanute, Kan., a town with fewer than 10,000 people, I cruised so often that I think I knew every winding road, picturesque alley, dusty pig trail, unusual pet, flock of birds, unowned dog, field of cows or construction site within 30 miles.

Like the staffs of small newspapers with few people and many pages to fill, we relied so heavily upon enterprising to fill our cover pages that anything daring to move between 8 and 10 a.m. was likely to end up on the front page of the *Chanute Tribune* – and often did. Even though it is often overused, cruising remains a profitable method for finding feature pictures. It gets you out of the office and onto the streets where life is happening.

Cruising also is an excellent way to learn a city or county, while providing an opportunity to scout for backgrounds that can be used for controlled pictures like food, fashion or portraits.

Here are three suggestions for making cruising more successful:

• **Start early**, before work if need be, and stay late whenever possible. Alternate the times you cruise for pictures. Life is different at 5 a.m. than it is at 3 p.m.

• **Walk instead of drive.** You won't cover as much territory, but you'll cover it more thoroughly. This will give you a close-up, personal perspective on your environment and force you to interact with people – something that is lost in driving. This also should help you avoid shooting every enterprise picture with a long lens from your car window.

• **Alter the areas and the environment you cruise in**. Plan several routes that lead you across town. Try capturing pictures from a cross-section of your readership – geographically, economically and ethnically.

Cruising is indeed a viable tool and a method of enterprising to be exploited, but it should never be a substitute for proper planning. Instead, it should be one of many methods for finding feature pictures.

3. Featurizing the news

When the Supreme Court announced its decision to protect the rights of flag burners, editors and photographers across the country looked for ways to localize the story. The Ogden Standard-Examiner featurized the story with a picture of 67-year-old Ray Mortenson under a flag flying at half-mast in protest of the decision.

A seldom-used, but effective, method is **featurize** national or international stories.

You take a national story such as the economy and look for a way to illustrate how it affects your readers. For example, a national story about large banks closing some small-town branches because of excessive operating costs might generate a local story if one of those branches is in your area. If so, how will the closing impact the community? What will the bank president and workers do? Will they have to sell their houses, uproot their children from school and move away to find employment? With every question, there are real and important local pictures to be taken.

Localizing national stories personalizes the news. You put a local face and name on national stories such as pollution, the elderly, education, environment, labor, health and transportation.

4. Newsletters

One of the most fertile places to hunt for feature photos is in the pages of various club, organization or institutional **newsletters**. Most organizations have newsletters, be they the Pork Monthly or the Colonial Manor Report. These "house organs" keep their membership informed. Whether announcing upcoming events, honoring outstanding achievements or discussing internal problems, these publications are idea gold mines. Schools, hospitals, nursing homes, sports clubs, alumni associations, missionary societies, law enforcement groups, government agencies, environmental clubs . . . Literally hundreds of such newsletters exist, and most organizations would be happy to put you on their mailing lists.

By scanning these newsletters, you should be able to plan for feature pictures that often have a news angle. At the least, you will be better informed on the organizations and events that shape your community. That will naturally open other feature-photo doors.

By regularly scanning newsletters, you can find small but important events like this couple exchanging gifts during a Christmas party at a Utah nursing home.

Without a midnight call from a reader, I wouldn't have known about this poignant happening. After apologizing for calling so late, the man said he ran upon something I might like to take pictures of. I thanked him and immediately drove to the site. Less than a week earlier I talked with the man in a coffee shop and gave him my business card with my home phone number on it. I had asked him to call me, day or night, if he ever saw something he thought might make a good picture. He called me again a couple of weeks later with another tip on a picture.

5. Networking

There is no substitute for communication. It is the grease that lubricates any endeavor where people are interacting, and it is absolutely vital for successful feature hunting.

Through mixing with the community and talking with people about their lives, interests, hopes and dreams, picture ideas should flow like honey on a hot day. By talking, and consciously listening, you will hear about all kinds of treasures: unusual pets, touching reunions and other personal happenings that make wonderful feature pictures.

Most people want to get involved in the picture-gathering process, once they understand what you are looking for and how they can help. Suddenly, instead of two eyes searching for that prize-winning photograph you might have a thousand eyes helping you **network**.

This is a similiar tactic that many businesses, particularly insurance companies, use to get leads. At the end of an appointment, the client is asked for referrals – names of friends or acquaintances who might be interested also. The practice works well for salespeople, and it works well for good feature photographers.

When your helpers give you tips on pictures and see them published, they feel like part of the team. There is great satisfaction in being part of the process, and they are likely to help again.

To enlist the help of others, pass out business cards. Give them your phone number, maybe even your home phone. Convince them that you are hunting together and you appreciate their help. Not every tip will lead to a publishable picture. But, so as not to discourage your helpers, you might have to shoot a lot of giant zucchini, dead animal trophies and weird things in the sky at night,which will never see the light of print.

You never know from where a good picture might come. A seemingly dull tip can blossom into a prize-winning picture.

6. Follow ups

Haven't we all read news stories and months later wondered what ever happened to a particular person or how an event turned out? Maybe it was a story of an auto accident victim, a citizen who won a lottery, a local beauty pageant winner or a high school sports star drafted by a professional team.

Perhaps it was a tragic story of a young boy who had been pulled out of a swimming pool unconscious. Usually there is an immediate follow-up, letting readers know if the child lived or died, but what about one, two or three years later? What were the long-term effects of the accident? What is he doing now? How has his life or his family's life changed since the accident? Journalists sometimes are accused of covering only the tragedies in people's lives. Follow-ups balance your news coverage.

Following up on news stories fulfills the readers' natural curiosity about a story and provides you with an excellent opportunity to shoot some meaningful feature pictures.

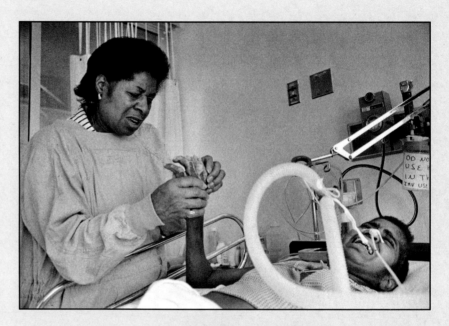

These two photographs were shot eight years apart. Airline flight attendant Barbara Baltimore was involved in a auto accident in 1977 and was not expected to live. Her mother literally moved into the hospital to help care for her daughter. Barbara lived, but her road to semi-recovery has been long and painful. I pictorially followed Barbara's story from 1977 until 1985 when the Sacramento Bee concluded the story with a multi-page layout.

7. Idea logs

A photograph of a cold, but dry, fisherman shot during a salmon run in Northern California is nothing spectacular, but the photo does have news value as a weather or sports feature. I noticed fishermen on the river while working on another assignment and jotted down the idea to be shot later when I had more time to wait for a picture to happen.

I am a habitual note taker. I write notes to myself on just about anything at any time of the day or night. I take notes at church, at lectures, even while watching television.

Sometimes I scribble notes on grocery bags, sometimes on coffee shop napkins and sometimes on my arms. I scribble down ideas out of the fear that they will escape me forever.

Later, I take these ideas and transfer them to a more organized and legible master file. It isn't uncommon for me to go through a complete spiral notebook during a cross country trip, sometimes using both sides of each page.

Creative ideas come unannounced, and, unless you have a computer in your head, you will never remember all of them. Keep notebooks for jotting down ideas everywhere – in your car, at the office, in your pocket and at home.

Who knows? You might want to record the time of the sunrise or sunset or the angle of a shadow at a certain time of day for later use.

Idea logs are a must when scouting areas for potential feature pictures. When feature hunting becomes tough, as it often does, you can refer back to your idea file, which should contain more story ideas than you have time to photograph.

8. Eavesdropping

Although I indirectly refer to this method throughout this book, **eavesdropping** is so critical and productive to feature photography that I have included it as a method.

Call it being a good listener or eavesdropping, it is really nothing more than people-watching in audio form. Thousands of people eavesdrop every day for entertainment.

Make a listening investment. Spend time at the local barber shop, coffee shop, feed store or mall. It is possible to eavesdrop without being rude. Listen to the gossip. Discover what the hot topics are in your town.

Pull up a seat next to a group of chattering students in a cafeteria. You might be pleasantly surprised by the picture ideas that can emerge.

Stopping between assignments one day to get a soft drink, I overheard some old men talking about a man who lived underground beneath a pile of tin and trash. It took me nearly two months and a few bribes to find Ivan Owens. Owens was once a business manager of a newspaper and a teacher in the Army before abandoning society. When I caught with him, he had been smoked out of his underground dwelling, but he still was an interesting story. After the story was published, an old friend who had lost track of Owens saw the article and convinced him to give society another try.

9. Study environment

Sometimes we look so hard for the unusual or the exotic that we ignore the fabric from which our community is woven. We travel out of town, often to far away places, looking for pictures that will interest our readers, when we ought to spend more time looking in our own backyards.

What distinguishes the place you live in from any other place in America? Is it a breathtaking mountain range and camping or sandy beaches and surfing? Is it windy flatlands of untilled prairie or national parks? What is your environment's claim to fame? Most importantly, how do people live within their **unique environment?**

Chetopa, Kan., claims to be the catfish capital of the world. In Gettysburg, Pa., one would have to be blind not to notice the battlefields and history. Corvettes are made in Bowling Green, Ky., and some famous caves are nearby. Every place has something that separates it from the rest of the country.

Ask yourself, what is important to my readers? What are these people about? What do they think about, dream about, care about? Where do they work? How do they play?

Is it farming, fishing, football, steel, electronics, lumber or tourism that affects your readers? Is it church and family that people build their lives upon?

Once you identify what your community is about, you will be better able to produce feature pictures that are important and interesting to the newspaper reader.

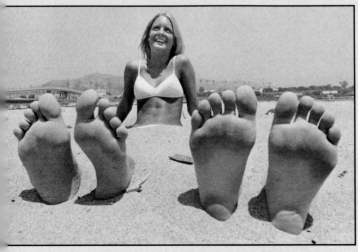

Top: What would Alaska be without fishing? Fishing is an important natural resource for the state that indirectly affects every citizen. Alaska is many things to many people, but to these hopeful anglers assembled on opening day of the fishing season, Alaska means fishing. Far left: Utah is known for Mormonism, mountains and winter recreation, like ice skating with grandpa. Left: California is much more than sunshine, tanned girls and sandy beaches, but all three are reasons why many flock to the Golden State.

10. Make a tree

Some people understand information better when it is presented in visual form through pictures and easy-to-read charts. One way to organize ideas and help you become a better feature photographer is to make a tree.

By making a tree, with the trunk being the main topic or event and the branches being subtopics or specifics of the event, you will find that identifying picture potential will be much easier.

When making your tree, always consider what the picture possibilities are before, during and after every event. This will give your shooting and publishing a focus.

To help you begin thinking about the numerous picture possibilities that exist at even the most routine events, here is a list of common events most newspapers routinely cover: Homecoming, Christmas, Easter, 4th of July, beginning of school, pre-season football and the big county or state fair.

Make yourself a tree for each event, and see how many branches you can fill with picture ideas.

Top: An overall view of a tree with the trunk being the main story or event and the limbs showing the various approaches possible. Right: A close-up look at one of the tree's main branches reveals the numerous sidebar pictures or stories that can grow from just one limb.

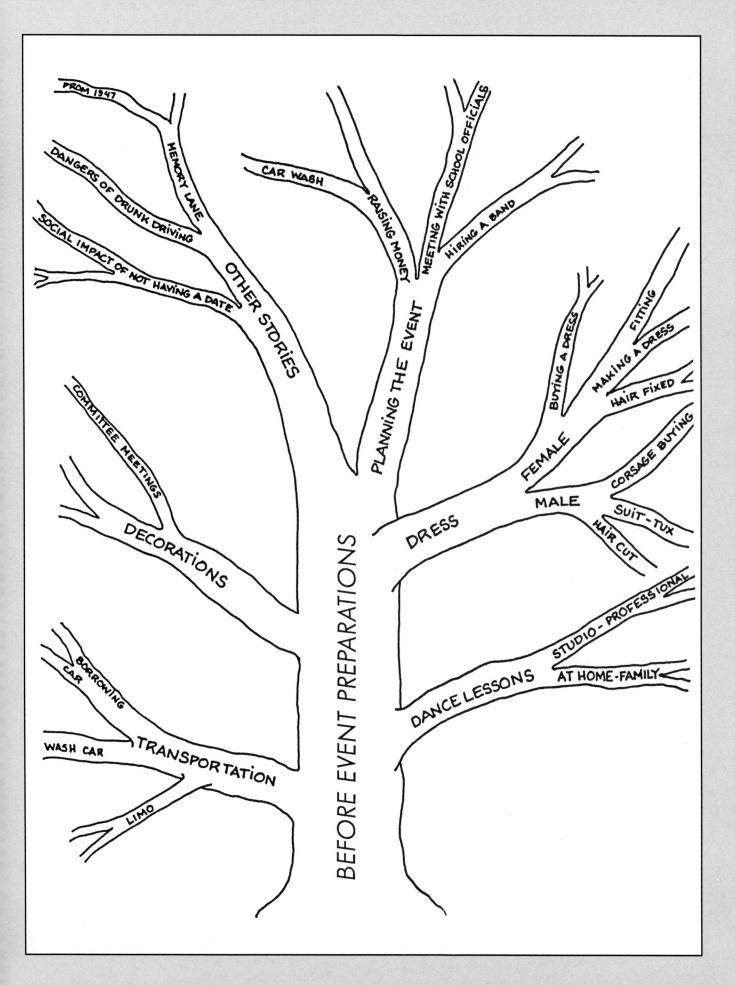

11. Search publications

Television, radio, telephone books, magazines, advertising brochures, newspapers – what do they all have in common? They are all **publications** overflowing with feature photo ideas and are fair game for the enterprising photographer.

One of the best ways to come up with a good idea is to borrow it from somewhere else, improve on it and make it your own. Just because a picture or story has been done somewhere else doesn't mean it cannot be done for your readership. After all, there are really few new ideas.

You will find that once you open up the doors of your imagination and let one idea lead to the next, you won't be able to stop the flow. Nearly everything – movies, television news, even a Sunday morning – will trigger picture ideas.

With news-type publications, look for upcoming events that can be illustrated. Look for stories that will provide follow-up pictures later or check for ongoing national stories, such as the economy, drought or environmental issues, that can be localized.

One of the most fertile areas to hunt in is the classified ad section. Study the help wanted ads for requests that have visual potential such as this one printed in the Waycross, Ga. Journal Herald: "Need immediately, 2 fox breeders for 6 months. Temporary position with 2 years experience in artificial insemination to train workers. Housing provided. $4 per hour." Who applies for such a position? Where is this fox farm, and how does it operate? Sounds like a feature picture story waiting to happen.

Curiosity should lead you to a list of questions that cry out for visual answers.

How about the personals? This is heading known for unusual requests, many of which can make for some very interesting pictures and stories. Here's one that grabbed my attention in the Arkansas Democrat: "Midnight rider, My hands touch a man of steel & melt him into syrup oozing from his shoes; I do mend broken hearts. Isis, Goddess of Egypt."

If that doesn't stir your visual curiosity and cause you to want to see what this person looks like, your clock isn't wound.

Under the heading **Horses** in the Lexington,

(Ky.) Herald-Leader: 1 male Dromedary camel, 1 reindeer. Call nights.

A few questions ought to arise from this unusual ad. Why would somebody have a camel and a reindeer? Where does he keep such animals? Does he have a wild animal farm? Who buys these animals and for what purpose? How would somebody transport them if he or she bought them? Just moving a camel sounds like it would make an interesting picture package.

Also under **Horses**: Horse dentist, teeth floated $20. 9 months 500-head experience. Where do you go to school to learn that trade? Furthermore, what in the world is is teeth floating?

When looking for picture ideas, the very first publication to search is the one you work for. I found an announcement for this Kansas baby contest under calendar of events for the 4th of July in the Chanute Tribune.

Of the ads I searched, perhaps the most unusual and interesting was this one published in the Ogden (Utah) Standard Examiner under the heading of **Situations Wanted**: Looking for a large, warm sun-lit room where I could let several large snakes crawl around for exercise on weekends.

An unusual request to say the least, and it didn't go unnoticed by the staff. A feature picture story was done on the man and his snakes.

But of all the publications that photographers search when their idea bank is empty, none is more popular than the yellow pages of the local telephone book. They teem with ideas just waiting to become feature pictures. They are wonderful for finding in-teresting people with unusual jobs.

The list of publications that can yield feature picture ideas goes on and on. The most important thing to remember with searching publications is that good picture ideas can come from anywhere – libraries, grocery store bulletin boards, in house publications, high school yearbooks, bus benches, the Bible, coffee shop placemats, matchbook covers, even bathroom graffiti.

Whether you check the Los Angeles Times, the Truckers News or the Pork Monthly, become an idea junkie and scan as many publications as possible. Do this and you should never be without a feature picture idea to shoot.

12. Police scanner

A moose running loose in town attracts attention and is news even in Utah, a state abundant with large game animals. Naturally, when people found a moose grazing in their back yards, they called the police. When that sort of news hits the airwaves, you take notice. Until I could get hooked up with fish and game officials, the scanner was the only way to monitor the animal's movements. The moose eventually was tranquilized and released back into the mountains.

Usually thought of as a hard-news tool, the **police scanner** also can be a valuable instrument to aid in feature hunting.

Law enforcement officials discuss police-related exercises, drills or general news events that make for interesting feature pictures that you otherwise might not have known about. These might include training exercises at the fire station or public-service drives such as bikers collecting toys for needy children.

Sometimes the conversation will reveal unusual happenings like pigs running loose on the freeway or a moose munching on the grass in a graveyard.

I have learned about preparations for events like rallies, carnivals, police competitions and drills from the police scanner. Any communication on any frequency can trigger a feature picture idea. Don't limit your monitoring only to the police channels. The police scanner is one of those communication tools that can offer some unusual feature ideas on slow days.

Chapter 4

What To Hunt

Specific types of pictures to hunt.

Some hunters thrive on chasing mountain lions or bears through the rugged terrain of the high mountains. Others find more pleasure trying to hit a darting rabbit in a creek bed or a hay field.

What to hunt varies from individual to individual, and so it is with feature photographers. Some feature hunters find the greatest pleasure in photographing kids, animals, light humor or social events like carnivals. Other are attracted more to personality profiles of eccentric characters.

First-time events

First-time events can be as simple as the first day back to school, as with this picture of Heather Foltz looking unenthusiastic about her first day of second grade at a Chanute, Kan., elementary school

Who hasn't watched children squeal with delight over their first puppy or fidget nervously while sitting in a barber's chair for the first time.

First-time events like these may be small happenings, but they are important moments in most people's lives. They offer great picture possibilities. Surveys show readers never tire of seeing them.

Don't limit yourself to pictures of children in first-time events. People of all ages do things for the first time. People in their late years can make their first trips to a major league baseball park.

Imagine the picture possibilities from a jet full of first-time flyers. There may be grandmothers on board who grew up in the horse and buggy days and insist that visits to the moon were done with trick photography.

How about photographing a first date, a teen-ager's first prom, a first day on the job or a first trip to Washington. D.C., to visit The Vietnam Memorial? The list of first-time events is as endless as your imagination.

One of the most important roles a photojournalist serves is to be a documenter of change. Shepherds have not always led their flocks to graze beneath high voltage wires or compete with factories for pasture land.

Our changing environment

An overlooked, but sure-fire, method of finding meaningful features when the hunting gets tough is to look at your **changing environment**.

The face of a community can change without us ever knowing it. Cornfields turn into shopping malls overnight. One day, you notice an old landmark like the post office has been leveled and a quick mart has taken its place.

These may seem like dry pictures, but they are important pictures, especially to people who grew up in the community.

There are pictures to take before and after demolition and renovation. Graphic images of steel bars going up or the sweaty faces of construction workers will draw attention to the changing city.

Visit city council meetings and with elected officials to find out about changes that can be photographed. Follow up on how people feel about their changing environment. Find out what has happened to people transplanted by change.

Keeping abreast of your city's changes will satisfy your picture needs, and it will update your readers about projects they may care more about than you do. Start digging a hole anywhere and people will ask, "What are you doing?"

Why not tell them?

People and their pets

Readers love pictures of children and their pets, like this one of Douglas Gregg, 6, of El Dorado, Kan., proudly showing off his blue-ribbon rabbit named Paul. Gregg's pet won the best of show in its class at the Neosho County fair.

The old adage says you can't lose with kids and dogs. There is a relationship between **people and animals** that is hard to understand, and even harder to define.

Whether through birds, dogs, cats or cows or even fish, we find great pleasure and companionship in our pets. And it seems the older we get, the more we care about our friends in the animal kingdom.

My father, who wouldn't dare let a cat or a dog in the house when I was a child, now has a little dog he actually lets in bed with him to sleep. He even takes her riding in the car and tells me not to use the term "dog" around her because she thinks she's human.

Yes, there is definitely something about the relationship between people and their pets.

Although I never intend to let a dog sleep in the same bed with me, I love animals and have considered what a different world it might be without them.

Look for pictures of people and their pets, and you will bring smiles to the faces of many readers.

Sequences

As most books require more than one chapter to complete a theme and movies need more than 30 minutes to tell their story, some happenings need more than one picture to communicate their essence. This is where picture **sequences** work so well.

A picture sequence is a package of pictures, usually shot in the order the events occurred, published together to complete a thought or event. A single picture might not capture the essence of the happening, but a group of images tells the whole story.

Although not published as frequently as they once were, picture sequences still can be an entertaining and powerful communication medium. They can also be educational road maps to instruct readers in many "how to" sequences such as building a birdhouse, fixing plumbing or, as early Life magazine once published, how to undress in front of your husband.

Picture sequences can be multiple picture arrangements, numbered for easy following. They also can be two-picture combos that share a moment in life as simple as a dog knocking over a trash can and licking his chops afterwards.

A single picture of this couple locked in an extra-long goodbye kiss at the Salt Lake City Airport would not be enough to convey the essence of the event, but a sequence reveals how long the kiss really lasted.

Many of my peers hate pictures with signs in them, but readers don't. Most people will read every sign in a photograph. Printed words or graffiti juxtaposed with people can create interesting contrasts. They can add to the mood of a picture and support the content or they can mislead the reader and misrepresent a subject. In this picture of a tired and hungry man at an Anchorage, Alaska, rescue mission, the sign lends support to the content.

Signs and graffiti

The image on the poster showed an unkempt, sickly woman sucking on a cigarette. The picture was eye-catching, but the combination of the image and the words beneath, "Smoking is glamorous," formed an unmistakable message.

Taped to a teacher's classroom window, that ad didn't make me quit smoking in high school, but it did open my eyes to the incredible power of pictures and words used together.

I learned that there is something magic about **life forms juxtaposed with artwork and type**, especially in the accidental arrangements of everyday life. I'm not alone in my search for this kind of feature picture. Some photographers specialize in shooting people and graffiti.

As our world becomes increasingly cluttered with ads telling us what to do or buy, the chance for interesting feature pictures that incorporate art work, type or graffiti increases as well. The more road signs, bus bench ads or giant billboards that are built, the greater the likelihood of composing or just snagging an interesting feature picture using **signs or graffiti**.

Look for ironic or unlikely arrangements – paradoxes, contrasts or statements about life. But be careful! What you say about a person, by pictorial inference can get you in trouble. There is a fine line between laughing at someone and laughing with him, and that line often is hard to determine.

Nature

My fondest childhood memories are interwoven with **nature**. I remember so clearly running barefoot through freshly plowed sod or lying in the grass watching as red tail hawks circled in the blue sky.

Those hot summer days spent exploring the cool, mossy creeks and shadowy canyons near my home are stamped in my memory forever and are an important part of what I am now.

As a child, I tried my best to catch and cage every creature that crawled, ran, flew or swam. At one point, I had more than 20 different insects and animals in jars and pens. Now, that intensity is directed to catching moments on film.

Out of those special childhood years grew a deep love for nature that has surfaced in my pictures throughout my career. Wherever I have worked, readers have been given a steady diet of photos from the great outdoors.

Some have argued that nature pictures don't belong on newspaper pages. Yet, when you consider how vital nature is to our daily lives, how can we avoid it?

Besides, nature is literally crawling with interesting feature photographs, and you don't have to wander deep into the woods to find them. Your back yard is alive with many creatures and pictures. Snails, spiders, ants and just about anything that wiggles can be fascinating when photographed with a close-up lens. After all, isn't that what photojournalism is about – taking a closer look at life around us?

Pictorials

When most people think of photojournalism, they envision breaking-news photos, big sporting events or political hoopla. Contrary to the beliefs of some photojournalism gurus, there is a place for pretty pictures in newspapers and magazines.

Those picture-postcard scenics, often referred to as **pictorials**, are a welcome relief from the blood and guts photos or political talking-head photos that often adorn news pages. Photographs of design, tone, pattern or aesthetic beauty have no deep meaning or important news value, but they are a breath of fresh air or a work of art within the news pages.

Shoot those late afternoon silhouettes at the lake, sunrises over fog-covered valleys, rainbows in full color and fields of spring flowers. These images give us a place to dream and a time to appreciate.

Ken Miller waits backstage for his next performance. Though clowning is an occupation that is visually loaded, it isn't always what it appears to be. Clowning can be a very lonely, and according to Miller, is a job that requires personal sacrifices, such as spending a lot of time away from home. "I've been calling home every night, but nobody ever answers," said the Whittier, Calif., clown.

Unusual jobs

What does it feel like to rip through the sky at the speed of sound or swim in a tank with killer whales? Have you ever wondered what it would be like to hand the bat to Harmon Killebrew, Babe Ruth or George Brett during a World Series game?

There are jobs, and then there are jobs. Most jobs are interesting in their own way, but they don't generate the curiosity about them that being an Air Force test pilot, a marine biologist or a major league bat boy does.

There still are many jobs that attract our interest and tickle our curiosity enough for us to want to know more about them. Some jobs are glamorous or romantic, like being an actor, cowboy or astronaut.

Race car drivers, wild animal trainers or under-cover narcotics officers interest us because of the danger surrounding them. Red Adair became mo-vie-star-famous for snuffing out dangerous oil fires.

There are jobs we want to know more about be-cause they are so weird or unusual. Being a night watchman at a junkyard, sitting in a tower watch-ing for forest fires, studying the chemical makeup of a dog's saliva sound as exciting as watching grass grow, but because they are unusually boring, they can be pictures.

Putting readers in another person's job so they feel danger, boredom, excitement or romance is a wonderful skill.

Weather

Weather determines how we move about, how we dress, our moods, even what we eat. When the **weather** becomes news, take the opportunity to record it visually.

Look for the obvious dark, ominous thunderheads rolling in, blowing dust, valleys buried beneath a blanket of snow, puffy white clouds against a blue sky. They offer spectacular images of the visible elements.

Try changing your shooting approach and concentrate on the effects of the changing weather. This approach usually will produce more news-type pictures of things like twisted power lines, swollen rivers overflowing their banks, uprooted trees or ice-covered roads.

You also can look for the positive side and beauty of the weather's harshness. Pictures of interesting icicles on the roof or green fields blanketed with colorful flowers bursting through the earth after a spring downpour usually lack emotion but sometimes best tell the story of the weather.

Finally, there is a way to capitalize on the human element by shooting the effects of weather on the individual. Capture images showing people reacting to or coping with the elements. Whether you shoot pictures of sun worshippers rubbing lotion on lobster-red backs or early morning commuters chipping ice from frozen windshields, strive to give readers a moment they can identify with.

Do more than reaffirm what readers already know. Show them something they have not seen or cannot see. Wow them. Involve them and humor them with your photographs, but never bore them.

Two ways to pictorially cover the weather are to show people coping with it, as the women in the top photo is doing while waiting for a bus, or to shoot the spectacular visible elements, like this Kansas lightning scene.

Special days

Christmas, New Year's, Halloween, Thanksgiving, Mother's Day, Father's Day, Memorial Day, Labor Day, Veterans Day, Valentine's Day, Flag Day and even Ground Hog Day are occasions our society marks for rememberance or celebration. With the sanctification of each of these days comes an excellent opportunity to produce interesting feature pictures. Don't forget **special** "religious" **days** like Ash Wednesday, Easter Sunday, Passover or Yom Kippur.

Anniversaries also have potential. Look for celebrations marking occasions such as weddings, birthdays or business milestones. There are anniversaries for achievements like ending wars or finding cures for dreaded diseases.

There are painful rememberances of tragic events like the bombing of Hiroshima or the explosion of the space shuttle Challenger. These memorable pictures usually are found on the first anniversaries.

There are exceptions, however, like the placing of the wreath each year on the grave of former President John F. Kennedy or Dr. Martin Luther King Jr.'s birthday. These anniversaries continue to yield many powerful images year after year.

Special days sometimes produce special pictures like this one of a slowdancing teen-age couple at a Valentine dance in Ogden, Utah.

Florence loves and cares for her doll, Mary, as if it were a real baby. She rocks it, talks to it, covers it up in bed and even puts real food down its plastic mouth. Florence is not a nationally known personality, but she is visually interesting.

Character profiles

Good feature pictures are found where people are found. Every city is rich with **colorful characters** who make interesting picture profiles. Everybody has a story, it just depends how it is told.

Interesting feature pictures may be no farther away than the person standing next to you in the grocery line. One of the great misconceptions begining photographers have is believing great photos come only from great events or far-off, exotic places. They think good feature pictures can't be shot in their towns. Nothing could be farther from the truth.

The old man whittling while he sits on the park bench, the weathered woman pushing the shop-

ping cart full of trash, the new mayor or the old judge – they are stories waiting to be shared. Some, if not most, of my favorite pictures have been taken at everyday events close to home. In 1987, Fred Comegys won the National Press Photographer's Association Photographer of the Year with a portfolio of pictures shot within 30 miles of his home in Wilmington, Del.

Right: Robert Miller gives his wife, Shirley, a kiss before dressing her to go out. The Millers soon forgot I was there and went about their lives.

Top: Robert pushes his wife, Shirley, across a busy street in Ogden, Utah. Right: Robert gasps for air after pushing Shirley up a steep incline; he has only one lung.

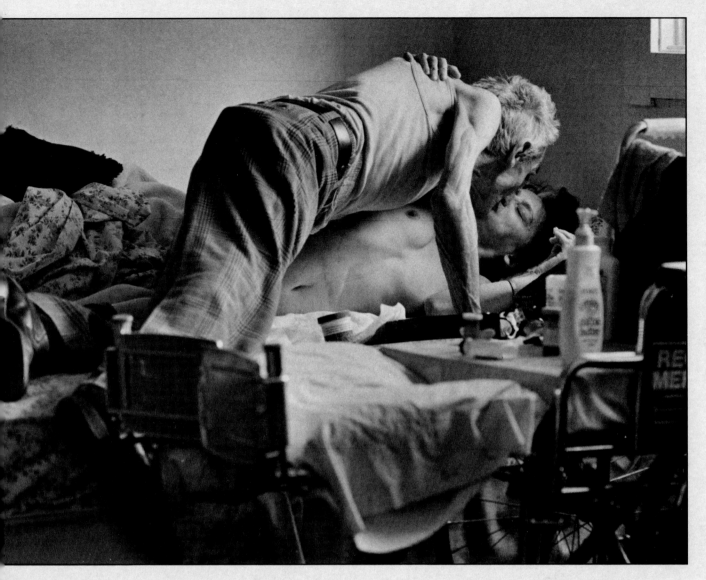

Pictures stories

This story about Robert and Shirley Miller started out as a single feature shot I found on the way to an assignment. It turned into a picture story. After shooting half a roll of film on Robert pushing Shirley across a street, I talked to the couple and discovered they had a wonderful story to tell. Of all the stories I've done, I don't think I have ever photographed two people who better embodied true love in marriage.

The couple met in a county home in Pennsylvania when both claim they were at the lowest point in their lives. Neither had family or resources to care for themselves. They fell in love and got married, even though they both were poor and in bad physical condi-

tion. Shirley, 41, has multiple sclerosis which confines her to a wheelchair, and Robert, 58, has respiratory problems because of a removed lung.

Officials at the county home would not let the couple live together after marriage, so they ran away to Ogden,Utah. The odds of Robert and Shirley having any measure of happiness were overwhelming. But, today the Millers are more than happy; they are deeply in love and satisfied with their lives.

The picture story should have a clear, strong theme. It should focus on one subject or event. Too many photographers fail miserably at photo stories because they either fail to identify a theme or they have no point of view – they don't know what they want to say. Andy Dickerman of the Providence (R.I.) Journal Bulletin said, "Today's young photographers come out of journalism schools with great ability to say something and nothing to say."

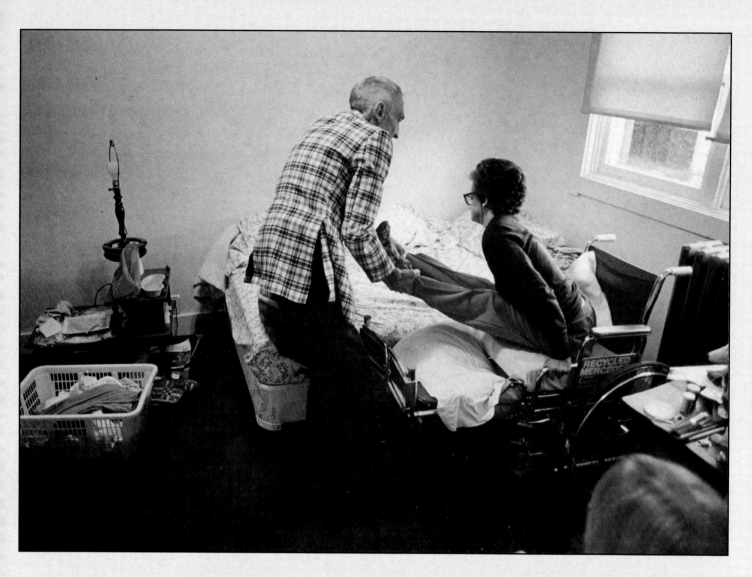

Above: Caring for Shirley is Robert's life. After dressing his wife, he swings her around to help her into her wheelchair.

Left: Bedridden much of the day, Shirley has a lot of time to think. "You've heard of marriages made in heaven," she said. "I think ours was truly made in heaven." Below: During a trip to the grocery store, Robert stops to kiss his bride, as he often does. "My wife, she ain't rich, but she's good lookin," the crusty and toothless Robert proudly pronounces.

The picture story is a wonderful tool for self-expression – a way for you to say "Here is something I think is interesting and important, and I want to share what I see and how I feel about it."

Study the event. Decide what to share, and then, please, don't be afraid to have a point of view.

Some people say that picture stories, like written stories, must have an obvious beginning, middle and end to be effective. Although I encourage students to try to use that approach as a framework, to be so rigid in definition is both foolish and impractical.

The more I study picture stories from the great story tellers, like W. Eugene Smith, the more inclined I am to teach students to look for openers or location pictures, and then follow their hearts and their imagination. To say that a picture story must have a beginning, body and ending is too confining and will result in students paying more attention to shooting for a formula than listening to their hearts.

The most important thing to remember when shooting picture stories is to establish a theme to have a clear focus to the story. There should be no wasted, or filler, pictures. Every image should add something to the whole, to give information or help convey the mood, while reinforcing the theme. There is a tendency in shooting and editing to be drawn to colorful or artsy images that have absolutely no relevance to the story. This is where the eyes of a good picture editor can help get you out of the weeds and back on the course.

By looking deeper, beyond the single feature for pictures that can develop into stories, you will provide readers with more insightful pictures and be a better photographer for it. Instead of shooting quick, superficial pictures, you will find yourself documenting meaningful moments that go beneath the skin of life to the heart of what we are as human beings. With picture stories, you can show others what it feels like to captain a barge down one of America's great rivers, fly a balloon across country, be on alert inside a military silo or cope with cancer.

When done well, the picture story is a powerful tool of communication, with each image supporting the overall theme or message of the entire story.

Picture combos

The two-or three-shot picture combination (picture combo) is used to give a little extra information, a slightly closer look at a subject or event.

Sometimes the only reason to publish a **picture combo** is that there are several good pictures from an event or there is a need to fill space. I am not an advocate of publishing photographs just to fill space, but neither I am naive to the difficulty of producing interesting stories on a daily basis, particularly on smaller publications. Ideally, you should use as many images as you need to tell the story – no more, no less.

Sometimes picture coverage of an event can be handled with a two- or- three-picture combination. A simple formula for combos is to shoot a wide establishing shot, move in and look for a good face or informative detail shot and then look for an ender, like this man sitting in race track litter long after the finish of the last race. This isn't a picture story but a three-shot combo of a day at the races.

Picture essays

Another multiple-picture presentation to look for in your hunting is the **photo essay**. Essays are not woven together as tightly as the picture story, but they are usually longer and more involved. The photo essay is a deeper look at a place, a culture or an issue. Most of the picture presentations seen in newspaper magazine stories or in long-term special projects are photo essays. No doubt many of the great photo essays, even some Pulitzer Prize winners, started out as single-feature picture ideas that grew into multi-page productions.

With photo essays, the theme can be as simple as the faces of newly born lambs, blossoming flowers or curtains blowing in the breeze or as complex as the apartheid issue in South Africa.

The way of the warrior.

"When we learn these new ways that bring strength and power, and have used them, then we shall rest" 5 Counties Cherokee Council 1966

Unlike the photo story, the picture essay doesn't usually have the strong narrative or opener- to- closer progression. Rather it is often a multi-dimensional look at a topic, such as this essay on the closing of indian schools because of the ceasing of federal sponsorship. The pictures represent a variety of issues and problems surrounding the closings.

Chapter 5

Hunter Ethics

The responsibility that accompanies the privilege.

There are two kinds of game hunters; the macho types gouge the land and litter the forest with beer cans and blood. They ignore hunting laws and shoot what they want, when they want. They give hunting a bad name. Then there are the sensitive sportsmen who appreciate the land and the life it supports. They value their rights and obey the laws of the land, taking only the game they are licensed to hunt.

There also are two kinds of feature picture hunters. The reckless shooters care only about themselves and getting "their" pictures. They believe that, in journalism, the end justifies the means. Then there are the sensitive photojournalists who see their jobs as privileges and approach them with responsibility. They appreciate their liberty to see and share, and they record life with care, so as not to harm.

When I began working for newspapers, I was a photographer, not a photojournalist. I was a high school kid in love with taking pictures and seeing them published. I had no idea of the tremendous responsibilites that went with being called a photojournalist. I was unaware of the importance of honest picture reporting.

It is the necessity for each of us to be reminded of our responsibilty toward each other as human beings that motivated me to include a brief chapter on feature ethics.

Photojournalists enjoy such great liberty to document and publish that they forget the responsibilities that accompany the privilege. Deadline pressure or a consuming desire for contest-winning pictures can twist a photojournalist's ideas about fair play, objectivity and sensitivity toward subjects.

Following are some trouble areas you should pay special attention to: setting up (staging) feature pictures or recreating missed moments, inappropriate behavior in gathering images, picture captioning and publication.

Some editors were opposed to publishing this photograph shot during a Boy Scout jamboree because they felt it poke fun at the individuals and there wasn't any important information being communicated about the event. The picture wasn't published.

Publishing

If you've ever been put to sleep for an operation, you know the feeling of helplessness and vulnerability. Your life is literally in the hands of strangers. You hope the doctors working on you will handle you with care, but there is little you can do to ensure that they will act responsibly. In a sense, the subjects of your pictures or stories are in a similar position. They, too, are vulnerable. They trust their names, images and character to you, hoping you will be sensitive and responsible when publishing.

Most photojournalists enjoy tremendous freedom to photograph. Just about anything the public can see, you can shoot with few restrictions. But publishing what you have shot is another matter. What you do with pictures once you have shot them often determines whether you are ethical or unethical.

An area of great concern in publishing feature pictures is insensitively printing humorous pictures that make fun of a subject's appearance or misfortune. Visually poking fun at people is morally and legally dangerous. You can do a lot of harm to a person's character by the images you choose to print. Published photographs have tremendous power to influence and shape public perception.

There is a fine line between visually sharing comical moments in life and making fun of someone because of the way he or she looks or acts. We all do funny things, most of which we wouldn't mind sharing publicly. However, there are acts like scratching itches or picking our noses that we would rather not see splashed over the front page of our local newspaper. Determining when a feature picture crosses that line between laughing with and at an individual is sometimes difficult. What may seem funny and harmless to you might be viewed as defamation of character or invasion of privacy by your subject.

When making a decision about the publication of a

humorous or potentially controversial feature photograph, the first question you should ask is what is the purpose for publishing the image? Does it tell an important story or communicate important information? Perhaps the main reason you want a photograph published is to get a nervous editor off your back or to have a clip to enter in a contest. Perhaps the picture is just a comic slice of everyday life and that alone is reason enough for sharing it publicly. Another question to ask yourself is, "If the photograph was of my grandmother or another relative, would I still support its publication?" Obviously this is not a scientific, fool-proof test, but it should help give you some direction.

Don't lose your sense of humor

In your effort to be an ethical photojournalist, don't become so paranoid about visually harming your subjects that you lose your sense of humor and discard feature pictures that are funny or slightly smell of controversy. Life is filled with humorous moments worth sharing.

A sense of humor is vital to healthy and balanced picture reporting. Often I have encouraged publishing humorous images, even those some editors felt squeamish about running. Few of the subjects I talked with later expressed any displeasure at publication, and most said they enjoyed seeing themselves in print. When there is a question of a feature picture causing harm by publication, why not be sure by making a quick print and showing it to the subject if you have time. See how he or she feels about its publication.

Be accurate and representative

Pictorial misrepresentation is the second area to watch out for. Your aim with pictures or words should always be to be as accurate and representative as possible. The credibility of documentary photography is in jeopardy. Too many picture subjects are disfigured or raped by image manipulation, wide-angle lenses and insensitive or biased picture editing. Worse yet, some editors use photographs as editorial weapons, editing images to reinforce their prejudices or sell their opinions. Sometimes editors are guilty of editing the news to fit what they think readers ought to see, rather than allowing readers to decide the truth.

Shooting angle, the lenses used, the moments you choose to push the shutter and, most importantly, what and how you choose to publish, can make somebody look guilty, stupid, silly or any way you wish to have him or her appear. With the right technique, you can make Charles Manson look like Mother Teresa. The pen may be mightier than the sword, but the image is quicker than the pen. You can ruin a person's character. I went to school with a guy who hated a school official so much that he used a fish-eye

This photograph of high school football player, Galen Shepherd i a classic example of a humorous photograph that many felt woul embarrass the subject if published. The picture was published, not only by the Chanute (Kan.) Tribune, but by many newspaper: after it went over the wire. After more than seven years since the picture's publication, I decided to find Shepherd and see how he felt about the image.

I reached his mother, Carol Shepherd first. She remembered th picture immediately. "We've had a lot of fun out of the picture through the years," she said. "We received copies of it from all over the country." But how did Galen feel about seeing his pictu published? Did it embarrass him? I asked him that question directly. "Not that much," he said. "I wish I'd had a chance to pull my shirt down and pull one sock up," he said laughing, "but I've never heard people say that much bad about it. When I saw it, I said, look at me! I'm in the paper."

Yes, the picture is funny. Shepherd's weight, his dress, his body language and expression all work together to make a humor ous feature picture. But the picture is also humorous because of the circumstances – the beginning of football practice, when mar players are out of shape. It is a real picture of everyday life, and sometimes life is funny. I admire Shepherd's ability to laugh at himself. Too bad more people don't.

What images you choose to publish shape the reader's perception of the event. If only the top photograph of Dick Morefield, a former Iranian hostage, reacting to a question with a funny-looking facial expression was published, readers might be left with the feeling that this press conference was light and funny. But that was not the case at all. As is evident by the other photographs, both Morefield and his wife were emotionally moved at recalling the terrible incident. Though the frame of Morefield looking funny is an honest image, it isn't representative of the event and would be out of context if published alone without an explanation.

lens to shoot the man's portrait for the school yearbook. The poor guy ended up looking like an anchovy.

The advertising industry uses images every day as sweet bait to catch buyers. They were the first to realize the great influencing power of pictures.

Know the law

When shooting journalistically, the First Amendment gives you great liberty to document and publish without the consent of your subjects. But, when shooting for commercial purposes such as for calendars, advertisments or other non-editorial or non-educational purposes, publishing laws change rapidly. In most cases you will need to get signed model releases from your subjects to safely publish their pictures. You may even have to pay a modeling fee. Stay current on publishing laws that deal with the rights of photographers, subjects and picture agencies. Don't take this matter lightly. Contact the nearest ASMP (American Society of Magazine Photographers) chapter for an up-to-date publication on photographic liability and responsibility. There are several good books about photographers' rights and publishing laws. Two such books are *Photography: What's the Law? by* Robert M. Cavallo and Stuart Kahan, Crown Publishers Inc. One Park Avenue, New York, N.Y. 10016, and *No Pictures, Please, It's The Law*, by Dr. Michael Sherer, University of Nebraska at Omaha.

At most newspapers, the pressure to provide good feature pictures to fill gray pages is very real. Sometimes under this pressure to produce, even the most ethical photographers are tempted to relax their publishing ethics and publish questionable photographs. It is a matter of temporarily satisfying a deadline and feeding that great monster called white space. In a perfect publishing world, there would be no gray pages that needed art. Photographs would be published because they were storytelling, visually compelling or because of the information they provide.

When printing breaking-news photos, the public's right to know is a strong defense for publishing. But with feature pictures, especially those that are humorous, the publishing ground is a little softer. Feature photographs perform a different role than hard-news photos, but that doesn't make them any less important. Don't poke fun at people with your pictures, but don't lose your sense of humor, either. There are publications that are visually depressing and unrepresentative of life because they refuse to print anything candid or funny. Those publications don't realize that when it comes to news and life, readers need to laugh as well as cry.

Withholding certain information about this photograph taken at the Vietnam Memorial in Washington, D.C., can change its meaning. Writing a generic cutline that does not answer obvious questions about the picture can lead readers to assume the man in the wheelchair is a Vietnam veteran. When a caption reveals that he was much too young to have fought in Vietnam and is not a veteran, the perception and value of the photograph change abruptly.

Captioning

There is probably no duty more hated by photojournalists than picture captioning. It is also the place most mistakes are made.

We usually don't think about cutlines when we talk about picture ethics, yet picture captioning is an area where the sins of assumption and omission are committed. If a photographer is not careful, a lot of damage can be done by poor picture captions. More lawsuits have resulted from what was said about a person in a picture caption than from the picture's content. People don't like to be misidentified or have their minds read. Speculating about what people are thinking makes them angry.

Too often, photographers don't want to be bothered with details like quotes, names or places. They just want to take pictures. But the day of the photographer who is not a reporter is past. Luckily, you don't have to be a good writer to be a good reporter. Good reporters know the story, ask questions and gather accurate information. Failing to ask the five W's (who, what, where, when and why) is simply failing to be a journalist.

Here are some trouble areas to avoid:

• **Photographers not gathering sufficient caption information**. Photographers sometimes see asking questions and collecting information as the reporter's job. They see themselves as "just" photographers, not reporters. Captions are not something extra. They are a part of being a journalist, and as important as shooting good pictures.

When you fail to collect complete, accurate information and expect a writer or copy editor to magically assemble a good picture cutline, you have left the door wide open for error.

Photographers often complain about inaccurate captions, but few ensure that cutlines are correct before publication. If you don't physically write the caption, be sure to provide enough accurate, legible information for a thorough cutline. Whenever possible, follow up on captions before they go into print. Not double checking cutlines written by others is a dangerous practice that can get you and your publication in hot water.

• **Making assumptions**. A quick way to get in trouble with captions is to assume anything – the spelling of names and places, dates, titles or relationships. If you are not sure about a name, ask.

Assumptions lead to misidentified picture subjec and misspelled names. People are said to be doir things in pictures they have never done, in place they have never been. We call ponds, lakes; gees ducks; and bison, cattle. And our ignorance goes public display.

• **Editors not taking captions seriously.** Readership surveys have proven that cutlines ar one of the most-read parts of a newspaper or mag zine. Yet captions are often ignored in productio Rookie reporters, copy editors or interns are ofte saddled with writing captions on deadline. Not a publications take captioning lightly. I've worke for newspapers that give photographers time at t end of their schedules to sort through their notes

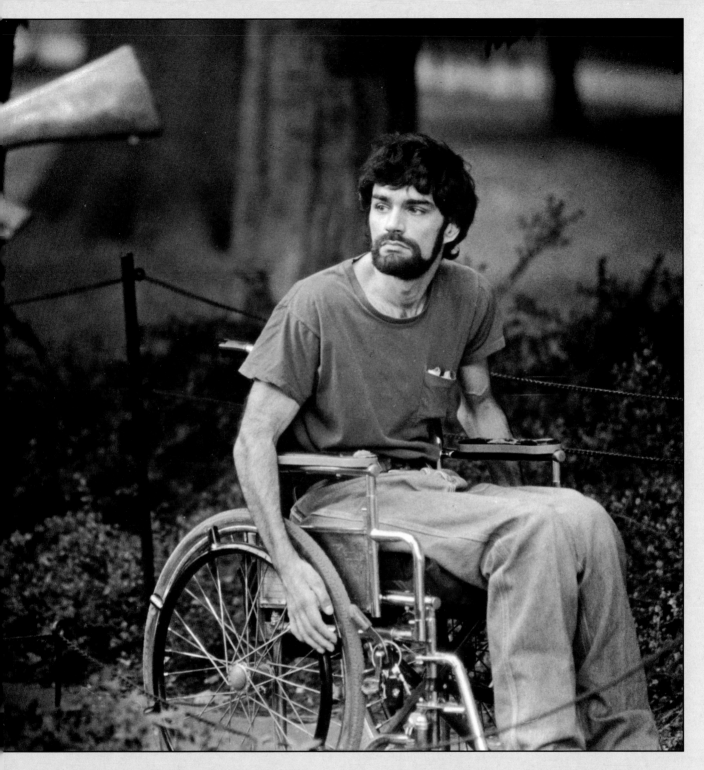

nd assemble accurate, thorough cutlines.
• **Intentionally omitting information so that picture will appear more compelling**. As unbelievable as this may sound, omitting information is done more often than photojournalists care to admit. Photographers entering published clips in contests have learned that pictures are sometimes judged more by the event they depict than by the quality of the photograph.

For example, a photographer shoots an emotion-packed moment at an automobile accident. The photograph shows a child who appears to be seriously injured being pulled from tangled wreckage. The uncertainty of the child's condition actually adds a sense of urgency to the photograph. As a reader, you look at the photo and imagine many things, perhaps even that the child died. But, if the caption reveals that the accident looked worse than it really was and that the child was treated and released, the perceived value of the photograph changes. Suddenly, the picture seems less important and actually loses some of its drama and urgency.

Recognizing that the perceived greatness of a photograph is often determined by the greatness of the event, there are times, especially in competition, when a photographer doesn't give complete information, particularly if doing so means minimizing the urgency of the photograph. It is simply a case of not wishing to upset a perception with the truth.

Staging

There are few joys in photojournalism greater than capturing a spontaneous moment. It is the ultimate accomplishment of seeing, timing and preparation coming together in a photograph. For the photojournalist, capturing a candid, story-telling moment is what a hole-in-one is to a golfer.

Unfortunately not all of what we see published in newspapers and magazines is real. In a world filled with artificial flowers, trees, foods and even love, there also are imitation pictures.

There are those who see no harm in setting up feature pictures or recreating missed moments. They argue that a photographer should do whatever is needed to make a feature picture interesting. Others disagree, insisting that to set up, stage or coach picture subjects is both unethical and a disgrace to the name of photojournalism.

There is nothing inherently wrong with coaching picture subjects or even setting up pictures. With most types of photography, even some aspects of news photography, the greater the photographer's

Top: The late Marlin Perkins shaking paws with a stuffed beaver is a candid moment. If it were a portrait I would have cleaned up the the busy background and lit it better, instead I waited about 15 minutes crouched in the corner for Perkins to pass by the beaver. To coach or pose a picture like this would be unethical. Spontaneous pictures, even with busy backgrounds, are better than fabrications that are perfectly composed. A group photo of Perkins with the staff and friends of an Ogden, Utah, nature center is obviously posed. There is no deception taking place; what you see is what you get.

ability to arrange and direct the subjects or lighting of the picture, the better the photographer is considered to be. In portraiture, group shots, food or fashion, it is necessary to arrange the subjects and "make" the picture. With this type of photograph there is no question if the picture really happened. There is no intent to deceive, and therein lies the key to determining right or wrong.

But when we, as journalists, set up, stage, recreate, cut and paste or electronically manipulate pictures and present them to the reader as real, candid or found happenings, we are attempting to deceive them. If the content of a photograph is not what it appears to be, but is a fabrication or illustration, the reader somehow deserves to know.

As unbelievable as it sounds, there are editors who actually encourage photographers to make up feature pictures, even to the point of giving them picture scripts to shoot for. I wonder if those same editors would encourage, or even tolerate, reporters fabricating stories or making up quotes. Sadly, there remains a double standard for words and pictures in many publications.

Wrong perceptions

A primary reason many see no harm in setting up feature pictures is that they have a wrong perception of feature pictures. They see feature photographs as fluff and fillers, and not as important as "news" pictures. They do not hold them up to the same ethical standards as news pictures. But in a very real sense, all spontaneous pictures – whether hard-news, sports or features – are news pictures.

Many news publications have all but abandoned documentary photojournalism, seeking instead to print colorful, posed, environmental portraits. They electronically build pictures from parts of other pictures – a blue sky from this one, green grass from that one. These pictures are easier to get and cheaper to produce because you don't have to wait for the pictures to happen. You make them happen in the most scenic places with the right light and just the right colors. It's a matter of economics taking precedence over substance.

Important distinctions

It is vital to distinguish between setting up a spontaneous-looking feature picture and arranging an obviously posed picture. Failing to understand the difference will do great harm to your confidence and cause you to shoot tenatively, without style or natural rhythm. For many years I operated from a position of uncertainty. I was so afraid of ethical violation that I allowed

fear to choke my shooting style and nearly kill my creativity. I missed wonderful moments that would have made good pictures because I was apprehensive about even asking someone to move out of my shot.

I see this same uncertainty in students. Some of them are so shackled by the fear of being accused of staging, they won't direct the subject of a portrait. This can cause serious problems in a business where a photographer is expected to work with and arrange subjects daily. Photojournalism educators are partly to blame for this insecure shooting approach because we tell students what is right or wrong, instead of teaching them to think for themselves. In our zeal for accuracy and honest picture reporting, we sometimes scare students away from nurturing their individual creativity.

I have operated from both benches as a feature photographer – from the liberal coaching and staging of photos early in my career, to the purist – "I won't move an ash tray out of a food shot" – approach for the majority of my life. Now, I operate somewhere in between. I don't believe in setting up or posing spontaneous-looking pictures and passing them off as candid moments, but I am not afraid to ask someone to move out of my shot either.

It's a tough call

It is not always easy to determine how far you can go in coaching picture subjects before your actions become unethical. But when you catch yourself using terms like "do this," "pretend like" or "act like," it is a pretty good bet you have stopped documenting and started staging.

Be careful! There probably is as great a danger of becoming a rigid, self-righteous, ethical fanatic as there is in becoming a "no-holds-barred" photographer. Don't become unrealistic and force your personal code of ethics on other photographers. It can be a long fall from the throne. There are many types of feature photographs, and just as many techniques that can be employed in shooting. When shooting for a journalistic publication, you should always have a goal to shoot factual, honest images with the least amount of interference or alteration. Few things undermine the credibility of a documentary photographer faster than fabricating candid-looking pictures and publishing them as found, spontaneous moments.

Strive to shoot honest images. You might not win as many photo contests, because choreography is hard to compete with. There will be days when you return to the office empty-handed or with less- than- perfect pictures, but when you do get those candids moments on film, the victory will be sweeter because you did it honestly.

After arriving at a serious automobile accident in Utah where other staff photographers were already present, Larry French stops shooting and helps emergency crews. A photographer's primary role is to document and not become part of the news, but we should always be human beings first and photographers second. If it comes down to saving a life or getting a great picture, I hope most photographers would value life more than any photograph.

Shooting behavior

Nothing is more unbecoming or harmful to journalism than insensitivity toward the rights and feelings of others. In a high-profile job like journalism, the way we treat others is critical in shaping public opinion about our profession. You often will be the only direct contact many people will ever have with the media. Your behavior while gathering the news may determine the lasting impressions people have of journalism. Unfortunately, there are journalists who are so enamored with themselves and their jobs that they see themselves as some kind of a privileged class. They view their subjects more as objects than as fellow human beings.

Operating with a "get out of my way" approach, without regard for the vulnerability of the subject or the fragility of the situation, is unacceptable behavior. Sometimes failing to read a situation can be as harmful as trespassing or stealing.

A case of insensitivity

One of the most crass acts of insensitivity I have ever seen came early in my career while I was covering the funeral of a 16-year-old high school student. The young woman, who had leukemia, died suddenly after a bone marrow transplant. It was a tense time as family and friends assembled for an oceanside memorial. Most were still in shock. It was a delicate and potentially explosive situation needing discretion, slow movements and restraint by the media.

I watched as other photographers, like me, kept a low profile with cameras by their sides. No one dared to venture in front of relatives seated on the front row. It was one of those times that it would have been wrong to intrude on the family's privacy.

Just as the services were about to begin, a car screeched up and a television reporter and a cameraman jumped out. What followed was painful to witness. The reporter, already a spectacle for showing up late, strode up through the gathering like an actress about to receive an Oscar. Chin up and high-stepping, she led the photographer like a dog on a leash. She bolted into that forbidden zone – the space that the rest of us determined was sacred and private. Then the situation got ugly. Totally oblivious to the mood of the event, the reporter stuck a microphone in the grieving mother's face.

I wanted to dig a hole and hide from being in the same profession as this reporter. With a microphone stuck in her face and a television camera lens fixed less than four feet from her, the weeping mother hysterically waved her arms and pleaded to be left alone. Finally, a relative came to the grieving mother's aid and calmly asked the reporter and photographer to leave. But the reporter held her ground and belted out in a defiant voice, loud enough for everyone in attendance to hear, "I have the right to be here. I am with the press." It was a sad day for journalism. No doubt, hearts were poisoned against the media that day.

A legal act can be unethical

Legally, the reporter and photographer had broken no laws. They had a constitutional right to cover the event, but they violated the moral law of dignity every human being deserves. Journalists can operate within the Constitution and still be harmfully wrong. The difference often comes down to the rights we choose to exercise and when, where or how we use them.

Some photographers justify aggressive behavior in picture gathering by saying that journalists must be aggressive and detached to do their job well. Many argue that such behavior is the sign of a healthy and competitive spirit. But there is no justification for arrogance or apathy in photojournalism. Contrary to some schools of journalistic thought, you don't have to be calloused or arrogant to be a good journalist. You can feel empathy for your subjects without compromising anything. It is possible to be aggressive without being arrogant, to be caring but still objective and sensitive to the rights and needs of others.

There are no laws or even professional ethical codes that can dictate when to lift your camera, push forward or back off. There is a greater law photojournalists should follow – the law of respect for the rights and dignity of our fellow man. Referred to as the "Golden Rule Approach" to ethics, our creator's teaching of "do unto others as you would have them do unto you" remains one of the best behavior guides in photojournalism.

Ways of The Woods

Some final words of wisdom

The eyes of a young buck deer and those of a hunter lock as the two stop and stare at one another. All is not as it seems, though. The deer, Bambi was raised by David Burdeau of Urbana, Kan. Although he has been returned to the wild, Bambi still enjoys following Burdeau as a partner and companion.

Even though I was on vacation to get away from shooting pictures for a few days, I couldn't pass the opportunity to have some fun and shoot a few pictures of my children, Bergen, left and Charbonee with this sign in Idaho. Fun pictures become more precious as the years pass.

Take time to shoot fun pictures

Have fun. There is no more important advice I can give you for a satisfying career in photojournalism than to make time to have fun with photography.

Most of us get so tangled up with deadlines, trying to make a living or advancing our careers, we fail to enjoy photography. If you are not careful, something you once loved and enjoyed will turn into something you dread.

Make time to shoot pictures for yourself, without worrying if your time is covered by a day rate or if your pictures will meet some editor's needs. Get lost in the pure joy of seeing and recording what

you believe is important. Photograph what you enjoy. Take the kind of pictures that probably got you interested in photography in the first place.

When I feel the passion for photography fading, I shoot fun pictures of my kids, animals at the zoo, country scenics or snapshots of friends. These pictures will never hang in a gallery, but they are priceless to my mental health.

Photography can be such a pleasurable affair. Don't allow its pleasures to get lost in the seriousness of making a living or the soberness of always trying to shoot award-winning images. Have fun.

Shooting approach

Occasionally students will question me about the physical approach to shooting feature pictures. They ask, "Do you sneak up on people and shoot before they realize you are there or ask permission first before taking pictures?" For me, a shoot-first-and-ask questions-later approach often works best. But shooting approach is such an individual thing that no two photographers will have the same. It's wise to use what works under the circumstances.

There are four basic techniques I have seen photographers use. The **first** is to be inconspicuous, or to sneak up on people as some like to call it.

This technique ensures candid pictures but does involve risk, especially when photographing the children of puzzled and frightened parents. When children are involved, it is best to let parents or guardians know what you are doing before you start shooting. This can be done non-verbally with a reassuring look or display of your camera equipment.

Most of my feature photos are shot with the candid approach. I try to avoid asking permission when I don't need it. Asking permission when you don't need to often gives subjects a chance to say no.

The **second** technique is to pick a spot where peo-

ple are likely to congregate and let the people come to you. With this approach, you are more likely to blend with the environment and people are not as likely to be alarmed by your presence if you were there first. Waiting for subjects and pictures to come to you is less intimidating to subjects than hearing screeching car tires and seeing a blur jump out of a car and slink between the trees like soldier in combat.

The **third** approach is to find something interesting then ask permission to shoot, while hoping whatever was visually interesting remains so. You hope that there are still moments happening and that your presence doesn't cause such a scene that people quit what they were doing or start mugging for the camera. This approach usually throws cold water on any real moments. Once people spot photographers, they either run and hide or start acting. There are times, however, when this technique is the only ethical way to shoot.

The **fourth** approach, which is practiced too commonly, is to grab a roll of color film, a kid, a red sweater and find some colorful leaves and start creating. Creating pictures and passing them off as real-life has no place in journalism, period!

Thinking they had found a pleasant spot to be alone in a Ventura, Calif., park, this couple has their passion abruptly inter-
rupted by two playful children. Meanwhile, unbeknown to any of the characters in this scenario, I was documenting the
happening with a long lens. Keeping a distance and remaining inconspicuous is often the only way to record real images
of real life.

Final hunting suggestions

Don't limit your subject matter. Everything, and I mean everything, is a potential feature picture. How we are born and how we die and everything in between that speaks of our humaneness.

A reader in Kansas once paid me a compliment without knowing when in a letter to the editor she wrote, "Nothing is sacred from Mr. LaBelle's cameras. He shoots everything from the womb to the tomb." The sensitivity of a subject should never determine if, but rather how, a story will be handled pictorially.

Go where people gather. Hunt at malls, parks, swimming pools or anywhere crowds gather to increase your odds of snagging good feature pictures.

When you find yourself scratching your head for a new angle, try projecting yourself. Ask, "where would I be and what I be doing right now if I were 10 years old?" You might be surprised at how many pictures you can find. Remember, you are a hunter. You need to think like your quarry.

Look beyond the assignments you are assigned to shoot. Spend some time looking off the field and into the stands, parking lots, locker rooms or consession booths. Annual events can become dull for the photographer and the reader, especially if the same picture of the same people, doing the same thing is published year after year. Beat the annual-event doldrums of parades, festivals and chamber of commerce banquets by challenging yourself to shoot something different this year.

Take a few risks. Try shooting at different times of day or at night. One annual event many photographers get saddled with shooting in small towns is the blood drive. I remember being sent to shoot an annual blood drive in Chanute, Kan. It offered the usual cliche pictures of people squeezing little rubber balls, waiting their turn or wincing as the needle punctures the skin. But I was determined after shooting dozens of these blood drives in my career to find a different picture. On my knees, I found a perspective that I had not noticed before. Not everyone was pleased with the picture I shot to represent the event, and some were even outraged and wrote the newspaper in protest but the photograph looking up a donor's nose was definitely different and didn't go unnoticed. Bend your knees, crawl on your belly, climb a ladder or a pole to get something different. For your mental health, don't shoot the same things

Always be on the lookout for feature pictures that can be used on news pages or held to accompany stories. When rain delayed a game between the Kansas City Royals and the Minnesota Twins just as baseball's hottest hitter was coming to the plate, I saw a bit of irony in the moment. Rod Carew was trying to become the first man since Ted Williams to hit .400 only to have a rainstorm cool off his bat. At the Chanute Tribune, we used an action picture of the game the following day and held this picture to go with a feature story on Carew.

you shot last year.

Start early and stay late. Finding unique feature pictures means observing life at different times of the day. You might be surprised to learn that life looks very different at 6 a.m. than it does at 3 p.m. You might discover a life out there you never knew existed. Remember, capturing interesting feature pictures means rolling out of bed and examing life before the crack of noon.

A Kansas farmer leaves tracks in the newly fallen snow as he goes to the barn at 3a.m. to check on a cow ready to give birth. I slept on the man's kitchen floor so I would wake up each time he made a trip to the barn. To get this picture, I ran out without my shoes and climbed a utlitily pole. The angle helped capture the mood of the event.

Dave LaBelle began his photojournalism career at the Ventura County (Calif.) Star-Free Press as a weekend sports shooter and lab man while still in high school. During his 20-year career, Labelle has worked for nearly 20 newspapers and magazines in eight states, including the Anchorage Times, San Bernardino Sun-Telegram, Chanute Tribune, Ogden Standard Examiner and the Sacramento Bee.

LaBelle's love for feature photography and his ability to hunt out feature ideas has helped him win many awards, including two Pulitzer Prize nominations in feature photography. He was National Press Photographers Association Region 10 Photographer of the year at age 19, an honor he repeated the next two years while working at various California newspapers.

He was runner-up to W. Eugene Smith for the Nikon World Understanding Award in 1974 and runner-up for the NPPA Photographer of the Year Award in 1979.

LaBelle joined the journalism faculty at Western Kentucky University in 1986 as photojournalist-in-residence. Under the guidance of photojournalism sequence coordinator, Mike Morse, Western's reputation as one of the top photojournalism programs in the country was enhanced.

Since LaBelle's addition to the faculty, Western students have won the annual William Randolph Heart Photojournalism Championship three times while capturing the newly instituted Intercollegiate Photojournalism Competition the first two years it has been given.

LaBelle has served as a judge for the 47th annual Pictures of The Year competition, and has been a popular seminar speaker for such photojournalism conferences as The Pittsburgh Conference, The Atlanta Seminar on Photojournalism, The Southern Short Course and the National Press Photographers Associations Flying Short Course.

In 1991 the National Press Photographers Association honored Dave LaBelle with the Robin F. Garland Award for photojournalism education.

The End